Animals IN and OUT

amicus
readers

Mankato, Minnesota

by Beth Bence Reinke

Ideas for Parents and Teachers

Amicus Readers let children practice reading informational texts at the earliest reading levels. Familiar words and concepts with close photo-text matches support early readers.

Before Reading
- Discuss the cover photo with the child. What does it tell him?
- Ask the child to predict what she will learn in the book.

Read the Book
- "Walk" through the book and look at the photos. Let the child ask questions.
- Read the book to the child, or have the child read independently.

After Reading
- Use the photo quiz at the end of the book to review the text.
- Prompt the child to make connections. Ask: *What are some other animals that are either in or out?*

Amicus Readers are published by Amicus
P.O. Box 1329, Mankato, MN 56002
www.amicuspublishing.us

Library of Congress Cataloging-in-Publication Data

Reinke, Beth Bence.
  Animals in and out / Beth Bence Reinke.
    pages cm. -- (Animal antonyms)
  ISBN 978-1-60753-501-0 (hardcover : alk. paper) --
ISBN 978-1-60753-532-4 (eBook)
1. English language--Synonyms and antonyms-
-Juvenile literature. 2. English language--
Comparison--Juvenile literature. 3. Animals--
Juvenile literature. I. Title.
  PE1591.R463 2014
  428.1--dc23
                           2013004496

Photo Credits: Sergey Uryadnikov/Shutterstock Images, cover (top), 16 (bottom middle); Shutterstock Images, cover (bottom), 1 (bottom), 3, 4, 12, 13, 16 (top right), 16 (bottom left), 16 (bottom right); Tom Reichner/Shutterstock Images, 1 (top); Heiko Kiera/Shutterstock Images, 5; Gerald Marella/Shutterstock Images, 6; Cathy Keifer/Shutterstock Images, 7; Kirsten Wahlquist/Shutterstock Images, 8; Leon Marais/Shutterstock Images, 9, 16 (top left); Cheryl E. Davis/Shutterstock Images, 10, 16 (top middle); Henk Bentlage/Shutterstock Images, 11; Ron Smith/Shutterstock Images, 14; Gentoo Multimedia Limited/Shutterstock Images, 15

Produced for Amicus by The Peterson Publishing Company and Red Line Editorial.

Editor Jenna Gleisner
Designer Jake Nordby
Printed in the United States of America
Mankato, MN
July, 2013
PA 1938
10 9 8 7 6 5 4 3 2 1

In and out are antonyms.
Antonyms are words that are
opposites. Which animals
are in or out?

Baby kangaroos ride in their mothers' pouches.

Baby snakes hatch out of eggs. They each have a little tooth to break their eggs open.

5

Woodpeckers peck
their beaks in trees to
eat bugs.

Chameleons stick
out their tongues to
catch bugs.

Baby birds stay in their nest. They are safe in the nest.

Prairie dogs poke out of their holes. They look for danger.

Red foxes and their cubs
rest in dens.

Lions sleep out in the open.

Penguins dive into the
water to look for fish.

They pop back out onto
the ice. They bring fish
to their babies.

Photo Quiz

Which animals are in?
Which animals are out?